The SOAR approach to environmental scanning represents a tremendous innovation to the strategic planning process as well as a generative integration of the appreciative strengths-based approach to building organizational capacity. Leveraging an organization's positive core, the SOAR process seeks to increase organizational capability and performance by pushing it beyond its existing boundaries to a more expansive state integrating strategic goals, objectives and activities (what we do) with values, practices and behaviors (how we do it). This creates shared purpose and meaningful engagement. This is a great book and a great contribution to the strategic planning process!

Thomas J. Griffin, Ph.D., Vice President, Organizational Learning, U.S. Cellular, Chicago, Illinois

The powerful combination found within SOAR of traditional strategic planning and Appreciative Inquiry has created a way for organizations to tap into new levels of strategic opportunity. Organizations have begun to discover that the old strategic planning methods of focusing on the negative aspects of the business lead to a downward spiral of counter-measures, instead of the upward spiral of potential opportunities and growth provided by SOAR. The motivational aspects of SOAR are also incredibly powerful, as employees and stakeholders find their voices resonating in the future plans of the organization. This makes implementation work. It would be a mistake to underestimate the potential of SOAR to dramatically change the strategic planning landscape as we know it. This is a very impressive book – great job!

D. Lynn Kelley, Ph.D., Vice President, Textron Six Sigma, Providence, Rhode Island

In today's world with its ever increasing speed of change, it is refreshing and hopeful to see frameworks emerge that will help us cope with change in a positive and constructive way. More than ever we need to discover our strengths, as only they will help us to find our true identity. All of us dealing with change will be inspired by the thinking behind SOAR – and the practical tools suggested – as described in this book. And as such, this book is an invitation to start using SOAR to help your community or your organization move in the direction of its strengths.

It was a great pleasure to read this new *Thin Book*.

Joep C. de Jong, Director Learning Solutions, BT Global Services, The Netherlands

D1545441

Our organization learned how to use the Quick SOAR described in this book and it exceeded our expectations. Not only was it an efficient planning tool, it was inclusive, engaging, flexible, and adaptable. Most importantly Quick SOAR was fun and inspiring. How many hospital meetings achieve that?

Karen Buhler, Acting Head, Dept. of Family Practice,British Columbia Women's Hospital, Vancouver, Canada

The *Thin Book of SOAR* is a practical guide for navigating a world of complexity with an easy to understand framework and questions that can change how we see the world from one of lack to one of possibility. It leads the reader to a new way of seeing based on finding strategic solutions, which often results in greater than expected outcomes.

Deborah Maher, Principal, Touchstone Consulting Group, Washington, D.C.

This is one of the best strategy books I've read. The SOAR framework and its approach build strength on strength in a practical proactive way. Strengths-based strategy puts right brain and left brain together with a whole brain-whole systems approach for planning in business, government, education, and non-governmental organizations.

Marge Schiller, Ph.D., President, Positive Change Core, Boston, Massachusetts

This book is excellent! It is an essential read for anyone looking to accomplish extraordinary results. It provides the framework for working with people in a positively deviant fashion that capitalizes on strengths and makes weaknesses irrelevant. The authors do an excellent job explaining what SOAR is and how to simply use SOAR as a whole system collaborative approach that brings out the best in people and their action plans.

Fadi Baradihi, Financial Consultant, Hantz Financial Services, Inc., Midland, Michigan

This is an excellent framework for engaging your organization – moving strategy from ideas to execution. Jackie and Gina have given us an inspirational, yet practical framework for helping leaders engage people in creating actionable strategies. A short read, but a depth of understanding that can only come from those who have been on the front lines. A must read for those interested in creating strategies and strategic plans that live beyond the annual planning meeting.

Mona A. Amodeo, Ph.D., Founder & President, idgroup, Pensacola, Florida

THE THIN BOOK OF®

SOAR

BUILDING
STRENGTHS-BASED
STRATEGY

By JACQUELINE M. STAVROS
and GINA HINRICHS

Authors' dedication:
We dedicate this book to our parents,
our husbands, and our children
who provide us the courage to soar.

Jacqueline M. Stavros, DM
(jstavros@comcast.net)
Gina Hinrichs, Ph.D.
(hinrichs@geneseo.net)

THIN BOOK PUBLISHING CO
Series Editor:
Sue Annis Hammond
(sue@thinbook.com)

Business Manager:
Rand Hammond
(rand@thinbook.com)

Designer:
Alisann Marshall
(marshallartsfamily@att.net)

Illustrator:
Nancy Margulies
(NancyMargulies.com)

© Copyright 2009, Jacqueline M.
Stavros and Gina Hinrichs. All rights
reserved. No part of this book may be
reproduced or transmitted in any form
or by any means without written
permission from the publishers.
Contact the publisher at the address
below or at info@thinbook.com.
Thin Book of ® is a registered
trademark of Thin Book Publishing Co
ISBN 978-0-9822068-0-5

ORDER FROM:
Thin Book Publishing Co
70 SW Century Dr
Ste. 100-446
Bend OR 97702
541.382.7579
541.317.8606 (fax)
www.thinbook.com

CONTENTS

What you are going to read

This *Thin Book* is about a profoundly positive approach to strategic thinking and planning that allows an organization to construct its future through collaboration, shared understanding, and a commitment to action. This approach is represented by the acronym SOAR, which stands for:

Strengths,

Opportunities,

Aspirations, and

Results.

One of the fundamental differences between SOAR and more traditional strategic planning models is that a broad representation of stakeholders are invited into the SOAR process. Stakeholders are the people who maintain an interest in the organization's success or failure. SOAR engages the stakeholders directly in a series of conversations to identify and analyze strengths and opportunities, in order to create shared aspirations, goals, strategies, and commitment to achieving results. While *every* stakeholder may not be able to participate, *each* stakeholder *group* is represented in order to:

• Identify and build on strengths,

• Connect to and clarify the organization's value set, vision, and mission,

• Discover profitable opportunities that the organization aspires to pursue,

• Determine and align organizational goals and objectives,

• Revise or create new strategies, systems, processes, and structures to support the goals, and

• Implement the plan so it guides every day decision making and actions.

Our assumption for this book is that organizations face more uncertainty now than before. The *before* could mean three years or three months or even three minutes ago, because we believe that the amount and speed of uncertainty is increasing. If you agree with this assumption, how do you deal with it in a way that doesn't paralyze you but instead gives you the confidence to act? Then, considering a global workforce on a 24-hour, 7-day work week, how can you ensure that each of those employees has the confidence, knowledge, and skills to act in a way that is aligned with the organization's values, vision, mission, and goals? This book is designed to introduce you to a framework to help your organization cope and thrive with increasing change.

There is a second important assumption in this book: Employees want both success and significance. Employees at all levels want to engage their minds, hearts, and spirits and feel as if their aspirations and achievements connect to their work. Employees seek organizations that understand that satisfaction and productivity are tied not just to wages and financial results but also to recognition, learning, and the ability to make a positive difference. They join organizations to have the opportunity to achieve goals that a single individual is unable to achieve. And, they stay with an organization, at least in part, because they perceive that their work is important and they are making a meaningful contribution. The SOAR process connects the dots between those individual values and organizational efforts.

We address the why, what, how, and who of SOAR so that by the end, we hope you understand the core elements and will have confidence to try SOAR.

Each chapter includes illustrations of SOAR in the for-profit, non-profit, social, and government sectors. The final chapter is our invitation to you to try SOAR, and we share several more snapshot illustrations of how SOAR is being used in

strategic conversations, strategy sessions, and strategic planning.

While SOAR is a strategic planning framework that can be used in small group conversations and in an organization-wide change process, this book is *not* a text on strategy. A deep understanding of strategic planning will *not* be needed to use SOAR. We will focus on the practical application that will help you use SOAR to develop a future course of action at any level to see how it generates the energy to carry out the plan. We invite you to SOAR and let us know how it goes.

— *Jackie and Gina*

Chapter 1 — Defining SOAR

... live with uncertainty but act with confidence.

— Dewitt Jones[1]

SOAR is a strategic planning framework with an approach that focuses on strengths and seeks to understand the whole system by including the voices of the relevant stakeholders. Focusing on strengths means that the SOAR conversations center on *what an organization is doing right, what skills could be enhanced, and what is compelling to those who have a 'stake' in the organization's success.* What we mean by "whole system" is that you create a more complete picture of a complex organization by accessing many different perspectives. One way SOAR does this is to reach beyond senior management to include others in the organization's actions. These stakeholders can be customers, employees, shareholders, board members, suppliers, volunteers, and communities the organization impacts. Furthermore, instead of viewing an organization as a machine with interchangeable and discrete parts, the systems approach tries to understand the integration and dynamics of the many relationships and interactions among people, locations, and functions. The whole system approach helps stakeholders see and understand at a high level how the system works and where their unique contribution makes a difference.

The SOAR approach integrates Appreciative Inquiry (AI) to create this transformational process. Appreciative Inquiry is a philosophy and organizational change approach that builds on the strengths and what is called the *life-giving* forces of the organization's existence, its positive core. David Cooperrider and his

Life-giving forces: Those elements or experiences within an organization's past or present that represent its strengths when it is operating at its very best. A life-giving force can be represented in a single moment, such as a particular customer engagement where service went above and beyond expectations.

colleagues at Case Western Reserve University developed the AI concept in the 1980's. AI engages the whole system in shaping the organization's future by looking for "what works" and "how to do more of what works" instead of the traditional diagnostic model of identifying and eliminating problems and gaps. The key question in AI is "What is working around here?"[2] SOAR creates a strategic thinking and dialogue framework to the AI process to guide the system during strategic formulation, planning, and implementation. SOAR offers a flexible framework to include the whole system or its representation instead of a more traditional top-down or senior management-only process.

What worked in the more vertical (and stable) world of the past was top-down strategic direction. However, to deliver innovation and respond to unremitting daily challenges, it is critical to involve all levels of stakeholder perspectives and ideas on an ongoing basis. The shift needed to gain that involvement is to connect the strategic planning conversations to participants' aspirations and values, something that SOAR does well. According to a *McKinsey Quarterly* survey of global executives, those organizations with the highest performance had a clear purpose, an understanding of strengths, shared *aspirations*, and leaders who knew how to unleash ideas with a results-driven process.[3]

Aspiration (n). 1. Strong desire, longing or aim, ambition.[4] Values (n). 10. The ideals, customs, institutions, etc., of a society toward which the people of the group have an affective regard.[5]

We have experienced how goals are achieved more quickly once this connection is made because there is increased energy and momentum to deal with challenges and potential barriers. Stakeholders are committed to making a difference because they see how their values connect with the organization's values. There is widespread understanding of how the collective effort moves the organization forward and benefits all stakeholders. This in turn maximizes people's commitment to contribute their hard work and insights.

SOAR invites employees to have a strategic conversation that is grounded in values. As a result, rather than trying to convince people to buy-in, the employees are motivated and inspired by the strategic initiatives that they helped create and that reflect their values. The function, department, and/or division goals flow into initiatives and projects that become the basis for individual performance plans. **The outcome is clarity and aligned action for each stakeholder.**

SOAR at John Deere

John Deere has been using SOAR since 2003. The results include increased employee energy and willingness to carry out the plans. Deere uses SOAR in a cascaded approach across and down several divisions, functions, and departments. SOAR links different areas and levels to the overall plan and helps each employee define his or her part in that plan. What engages Deere employees is the inquiry into Aspirations (the "A" in SOAR) which in turn inspires innovation and action based on employees' values and strengths. This works well at Deere because the company has a highly ethical reputation and a long history of putting the values of integrity, quality, innovation, and commitment into action on a daily basis. The SOAR framework creates conversations that align those values from top down and across a large global organization.

SOAR is also used to communicate sustainable value within organizations. *Sustainable value*[6] means that an organization considers how its core business impacts the planet and people while making a profit, which is also known as the triple bottom line approach.[7] John Deere does this by providing its customers with technologies that encourage effective stewardship of the earth. For example, the information technology used on farm equipment maps the land to optimize the application of fertilizers, herbicides, and pesticides.

The SOAR approach also nurtures a culture of continuous organizational learning because stakeholders who participate in the strategy conversations learn from each other and establish collaborative working relationships. **They share and create knowledge and also learn how to operate through the conversation.** The result is the ability to make decisions that support the organization's strategy and goals on the frontline and in the moment of providing service.

In summary, SOAR increases understanding of how stakeholder efforts fit within the organization's mission, vision, goals, and objectives. A strategic plan is not static; it can adapt quickly to a changing environment if stakeholders took part in the identification of organizational strengths and opportunities and are constantly scanning the environment for new ones. This stakeholder commitment can be the difference between achieving the organizational goals and missing the moving mark. A SOAR strategic plan is a collective understanding of the organization's goals, so that everyone at every level can make informed adjustments to decisions and actions when needed.

Now that we know something about SOAR, we can turn our attention in the next chapter to contrast SOAR with a strategic planning tool called SWOT.

Key Points of this Chapter

- Why SOAR is more suited to today's environment.
- How SOAR supports strategic implementation through the engagement and alignment of stakeholders in strategic thinking and conversations.

Strategic Thoughts

- Think about a time when your organization was most successful in adopting a different strategy. How important was stakeholder engagement and alignment?
- If you were to use SOAR for a strategy session or to create a strategic plan, who are the relevant stakeholders that you would want to include in the conversation?
- How might you start a strategic conversation that allows for stakeholders' aspirations to be heard?

Chapter 2   **What is Different about SOAR?**

The task of leadership is to create an alignment of strengths, making our weaknesses irrelevant.

— Peter Drucker

The standard tool of strategic planning, used for decades is called SWOT. SWOT stands for Strengths, Weaknesses, Opportunities, and Threats. Although SWOT can be used at any level of an organization, it is traditionally employed at the senior management level. SOAR is also used at the top level of an organization but seeks to include stakeholders at many levels. This is a key difference of SOAR, because it engages those employees who are generally not part of the strategic planning process yet can offer invaluable insights into strengths and opportunities of the organization.

SOAR and SWOT have a "both/and" relationship because SOAR leverages the strengths and opportunities from SWOT as a foundation and then adds aspirations and results. The diagram on the following page compares and differentiates SOAR from SWOT.

Comparison of SWOT / SOAR Approaches: *Both/And*

SWOT	SOAR
STRENGTHS • Organization's resources and capabilities • Basis for developing differentiating advantage	**STRENGTHS** • What are we doing really well? • What are our greatest assets? • What are we most proud of accomplishing? • What do our strengths tell us about our skills?
WEAKNESSES • Absence of strength; lack of resource or capability • Flipside of a strength; downside of focusing on competitive advantage	**OPPORTUNITIES** • How do we collectively understand outside threats? • How can we reframe to see the opportunity?
OPPORTUNITIES • External circumstances that support profit and growth • Unfulfilled customer needs, new technology, favorable legislation	• What is the enterprise asking us to do? • How can we best partner with others?
THREATS • External circumstances that hinders profit and growth • E.g., more competitors, changes to revenue stream, restrictive regulations	

+

ASPIRATIONS
• Considering Strengths and Opportunities, who should we become?
• How do we allow our values to drive our vision?
• How can we make a difference for our organization and its stakeholders?

+

RESULTS
• What are our measurable results?
• What do we want to be known for?
• How do we tangibly translate Strengths, Opportunities, and Aspirations?

Many are familiar with SWOT. However, if more information is required there are numerous resources available. Classic books we recommend are listed on page 45. **The goal of this book is to explain how SOAR differs and how you might consider applying SOAR.** The table below highlights the differences between the two models.

SWOT ANALYSIS	SOAR APPROACH
Analysis oriented	Action oriented
Weaknesses & Threats focus	Strengths & Opportunity focus
Competition focus – *Just be better*	Possibility focus – *Be the best!*
Incremental improvement	Innovation & breakthroughs
Top down	Engagement of all levels
Focus on Analysis → Planning	Focus on Planning → Implementation
Energy depleting –*There are so many weaknesses and threats!*	Energy creating – *We are good and can become great!*
Attention to Gaps	Attention to Results

Another key distinction of the SOAR approach is to identify and expand existing strengths and opportunities rather than drill down on problems, deficiencies, weaknesses, and threats. Dedicating the same amount of time to each of the four SWOT components means spending half of the time thinking about positives (strengths and opportunities) and the other half thinking about negatives (weaknesses and threats). This effort tends to cancel any forward momentum. Research has shown that building on people's strengths can produce greater results than spending time correcting their weaknesses.[8] Gallup Poll researchers Donald Clifton and James Harter report that in organizations where workers focus on their strengths, productivity is one and one-half times greater than an organization that focuses on weaknesses.[9]

People tend to look for problems and focus on weaknesses and threats before searching for possibilities. For example, one participant of a SWOT process described this tendency as follows: "Having used SWOT analysis for the previous fifteen years, I had experienced that it could be draining, as people often got stuck in the weaknesses and threats conversations. The analysis became a descending spiral of energy." Or, as another described his experience of a planning process deeply rooted in a SWOT analysis, "[the SWOT approach] gave us a plan, but took our spirit."[10] From our experience, drained energy and loss of spirit can negatively impact momentum and achieving results.

In SOAR, we focus on our strengths and opportunities, so that we can align and expand them until they lessen or manage our weaknesses and threats. **Weaknesses and threats are not ignored. They are reframed and given the appropriate focus within the Opportunities and Results conversation. Ultimately, it becomes a question of balance. Why not spend as much time or more on what you do well and how you can do *more* of that? What gives you more energy to take action? What gives you confidence to set a stretch goal?**

Data now confirms what we knew intuitively; positive emotions resulting from a focus on strengths can promote upward spirals toward optimal individual and organizational performance. Dr. Barbara Fredrickson's research in this area is clearly explained in her book, *Positivity.*[11] She reports that a ratio of three positive emotions to each negative emotion changes how your mind actually works. She defines ten forms of positive emotions including joy, hope, interest, inspiration, and amusement.

Adding to Fredrickson's work are the years of research by her colleague, Dr. Marcial Losada, analyzing how people talk to each other in team meetings. He codes and sorts the conversations into three categories: positive or negative, self-focused or other-focused, and the ratio of asking questions to defending a point of view. He was able to translate this data into a mathematical model that plots significant differences. Those differences are directly reflected in performance. High performing teams talk to each other differently than low performing teams. High performing teams are more positive, ask more questions, and are more focused outside of themselves (other-focused). These are also the characteristics of SOAR's strengths-focused strategic conversations. SOAR is a way to help people learn to have positive and other-focused inquiry.

Dr. Kim Cameron, a researcher from the University of Michigan, has reported on the affect of positive leadership on organizational performance. Cameron describes how a leader creates a positive environment through constructive and collaborative relationships. These types of relationships are described by two other researchers, Dutton and Ragins, as a "generative source of enrichment, vitality, and learning."[12] Cameron says that when people are "pursuing a profound purpose or engaging in work that is personally important, significant positive effects are produced, including reductions in stress, turnover, absenteeism, dissatisfaction, and cynicism, as well as increases in commitment, effort, engagement, empowerment, satisfaction, and a sense of fulfillment."[13] SOAR helps people connect their purpose and values to their work through the strategic conversations.

Cameron also reports that "high-levels of meaningfulness in work have been associated with positive outcomes and extraordinary individual and organizational performance."[14] An example in his book, *Making the Impossible Possible*, describes an effort to clean up a contaminated nuclear plant. The job was completed sixty years earlier than scheduled, $30 billion under budget and thirteen times cleaner than mandated. Over the years the stakeholders worked together, the once contentious relationships changed to become positive. Cameron attributes that to the fact that there was moral purpose and years of collaboration to transform this dangerous site to "a wildlife refuge – a safe environment for thousands of years to come." [15]

Too many wonderfully conceived strategic plans sit unused on shelves of organizations around the world. We believe that strategy should be a living, energy-creating part of everyone's job. Many of us have had the experience of being presented with a strategic plan that we were expected to implement, despite our lack of input into the plan. Because SOAR engages stakeholders from all levels to contribute their ideas, there is buy-in by those who must carry out the activities of the strategic plan. Because of this participation, it has been our experience that implementation time is significantly reduced.

From Average to Top-Performance

A regional office of a professional services firm used SOAR to engage all its employees and a few key customers with impressive results. Prior to using SOAR, the office was holding its own in overall global ranking but it was known as an average performer. It ranked 8th in total revenues and 12th in operating profit out of twenty-five offices. In addition, employee engagement and retention rates were low. With an annualized employee turnover rate of 36%, the office ranked 6th in the firm for retaining employees. The office was meeting expectations but the leadership team believed it could do even better.

The strategic planning team decided to integrate the SOAR framework by first including a group of forty internal stakeholders that represented the various positions in the organization. Within the next few months, all employees were invited into the strategic planning process. The managing director thought that building on the firm's strengths and engaging all the employees in the strategic dialogue would yield a positive impact on meeting client satisfaction, operations, and financial goals. His hopes were realized when the office was rated the firm's largest and most profitable operation, ranking first in employee engagement, client satisfaction, revenue, and income, and dropping the employee turnover rate from 36% to just 7%.

RELATIVE RANK OF THE OFFICE WITHIN THE FIRM

	YEAR 1		YEAR 2	YEAR 3	YEAR 4
Employee Engagement	6th	**S**	1st	1st	1st
Employee Retention	6th	**O**	3rd	1st	1st
Client Satisfaction	8th	**A**	8th	6th	1st
Revenue	8th	**R**	5th	4th	1st
Income	12th		6th	2nd	1st

Source: Chapter 18, Linking Strategy and OD to Sustainable Performance by Stavros, J. and Saint, D. in W. Rothwell, J. Stavros, R. Sullivan, and A. Sullivan in *Practicing Organization Development: A Guide to Leading Change*, 2010, Jossey-Bass.

How can you achieve those results and make strategy part of everyone's job? The next two chapters offer more detail on how to get started.

Key Points of this Chapter

- Compares and differentiates SOAR from SWOT.
- Shows the possibility focus of SOAR and how it can create greater innovation and energy for change.

Strategic Thoughts

- Consider how SOAR could be applied at different levels in your organization. How would the framework be applied at the top levels of the organization or for cascading and aligning to other levels?
- Review the questions in the SWOT and SOAR diagram on page 11. How would you rephrase the questions to suit your strategic planning conversations?
- How might you reframe a weakness or threat into a possibility, aspiration, or future opportunity that inspires?

Chapter 3

What is the Essence of SOAR?

Within our dreams
and aspirations we find
our opportunities.

— Sue Atchley Ebaugh

SOAR involves creating a series of *conversations* to gain a whole system perspective. This happens by involving those who are connected to each other by that system, including front-line employees, customers and suppliers, volunteers, regulators, and community representatives. This encourages participants "to think about the organization as a system whose parts are mutually interdependent."[16] The questions used in the conversations are designed to help the organization's stakeholders understand what happens when the organization is working at its best and how to apply that information to create a desired future. **SOAR differs from other strategic approaches because of the questions that are asked and because of who answers them.** Here are samples of questions used in SOAR conversations. The questions are first reviewed by executive sponsors or a "core" strategic planning team and then asked of the stakeholders.

STRENGTHS: *What can we build on?*

- What are we most proud of as an organization? How does that reflect our greatest strength?
- What makes us unique? What can we be best at in our world?[17]
- What is our proudest achievement in the last year or two?
- How do we use our strengths to get results?

- How do our strengths fit with the realities of the marketplace?
- What do we do or provide that is world class for our customers, our industry, and other potential stakeholders?

OPPORTUNITIES: *What are our stakeholders asking for?*

- How do we make sense of opportunities provided by the external forces and trends?
- What are the top three opportunities on which we should focus our efforts?
- How can we best meet the needs of our stakeholders, including customers, employees, shareholders, and community?
- Who are possible new customers?
- How can we distinctively differentiate ourselves from existing or potential competitors?
- What are possible new markets, products, services, or processes?
- How can we reframe challenges to be seen as exciting opportunities?
- What new skills do we need to move forward?

ASPIRATIONS: *What do we care deeply about?*

- When we explore our values and aspirations, "what are we deeply passionate about?"[18]
- Reflecting on Strengths and Opportunities conversations, who are we, who should we become, and where should we go in the future?
- What is our most compelling aspiration?
- What strategic initiatives (i.e. projects, programs, and processes) would support our aspirations?

RESULTS: *How do we know we are succeeding?*

- Considering our Strengths, Opportunities, and Aspirations, what meaningful measures would indicate that we are on track to achieving our goals?
- What are 3 to 5 indicators that would create a scorecard that addresses a triple bottom line of profit, people, and planet?
- What resources are needed to implement our most vital projects?
- What are the best rewards to support those who achieve our goals?

The SOAR questions are the basis for conversations held in small groups. This is followed by reporting to a larger group to create shared understanding. The small group to large group conversation flow works because participants have a sense of safety and a greater chance to contribute their knowledge and thoughts in the small group. By reporting to the large group, shared thinking and critical mass are created. This approach provides the benefit of both a small and large group and shows how SOAR is scalable. It can be conducted at any level in the organization and involve any number of participants in the same physical location or connected virtually.

Conventional wisdom holds that the most effective size for strategic planning teams is seven to twelve participants from the top levels of the firm. Now larger groups with participants at any level can be engaged with the use of small group breakout sessions and collaborative technology. There is no limit to the size of a strategic planning session. It is possible to have effective sessions with groups that exceed 1000 people! With the help of web-enabled technology the participants can be anywhere in the world, increasing knowledge and commitment across the global organization and significantly reducing implementation time.[19]

For example, Northern Essex Community College, which has multiple campuses in the Boston area, initially engaged a core strategic planning team of twenty people. The interest in serving on this team was so overwhelmingly positive, that the college decided to be as inclusive as possible and opened it to any and all interested stakeholders. As a result, another twenty-five people joined the strategic planning team. By the time the two-day regional planning forum was held, over 170 stakeholders attended. This included students, alumni, parents, administrators, faculty, staff, board of trustees, and community supporters. The outcome was a three-year strategic plan with a core value set, a clear vision, a mission, and a strategy incorporating six strategic initiatives and measures to lead the college from a no-growth to a growth strategy throughout the entire region.

Quick SOAR

The wide variety in the number of participants impacts the time it takes to answer the SOAR questions so there isn't any "standard" schedule. We have conducted many half-day to full-day sessions that we refer to as quick SOAR. For a quick SOAR session, the small group conversations can be scheduled allowing 30 to 60 minutes of dialogue on each of the four SOAR elements. Each group is also given five minutes to report out to the larger group. A sample schedule for a quick SOAR session is on page 21. No matter how much time you have available, the goal is to ensure all participants are heard and there is sufficient information and time to inquire, imagine, innovate, and make informed decisions.

The scalability of SOAR allows the framework to be applied in a quick SOAR or to a more rigorous and formal strategic planning process. A quick SOAR is especially suited to divisional, functional, project, and individual planning where alignment to the larger organization's strategy is critical. The quick SOAR objective is to conduct the conversations to create understanding of the local entity's Strengths, Opportunities, Aspirations, and Results. Participants leave with a clearer understanding of how their personal and local unit fits into the larger organization's goals.

A Quick SOAR Example

A director of a task force needed a strategy to obtain funding and create a youth leadership development program that inspired open dialogue, diversity, and inclusion. The director held a five-hour strategic conversation using the questions listed in this chapter. Here is a summary of the "answers" to those questions.

STRENGTHS: *What can we build on?*

Community presence in inner city and 10 mile radius

Peace walk celebrations

Youth peacemakers

Taskforce diversity

Young members and adult members blend

Attract leaders to speak to members

OPPORTUNITIES: *What can we do for our youth?*

Create a youth leadership program that advances our legacy

Partner with local and national youth groups

Send youths to president's inauguration

Leverage competent leadership team to design the best youth leadership program in the nation

ASPIRATIONS: *What do we desire to be?*

To be the premier catalysts for outreach to communities and their youth to develop leadership programs through our legacy of positive social change, equality, diversity, and education.

RESULTS: *How do we know we are succeeding?*

Funding is received for the Youth Legacy Leadership Development Program.

A vibrant and meaningful youth leadership program is created.

Youth are accepted from all over the city and there is a waiting list for next year's program.

Abundance of leaders are applying to teach, mentor, and coach our youths into effective leaders.

From this quick SOAR session, held in just five hours with fourteen people participating, the director created a proposal for funding the leadership development program. Within three months, the funding was received to develop the program. Four months after that, several youth attended the President's inauguration in Washington, D.C.

A more rigorous and formal strategic planning approach is called for when creating a 3 to 5-Year Strategic Plan for the entire organization. This is often a two to three day event. We use what we call the 5-I approach to engage the relevant stakeholders in a formal planning process to gather and analyze data to build a strategic plan. The 5-I approach is covered in the next chapter.

Seeing the whole and their part of the vision is how SOAR creates greater alignment and energy to move quickly to achieve the new strategy. For years, individuals have recognized the value of setting stretch goals or focusing on a desired outcome. Athletes and sport teams have used mental imaging as a standard training method. They picture themselves performing flawlessly instead of concentrating on the errors in their last performance. Why should an organization be any different? Getting the entire team to envision a shared goal or outcome shifts the conversation, thoughts, and mindset from "what's wrong with us?" to "how great can we be?" Jim Collins said in his book, *Good to Great*: "If you make a lot of money doing things at which you could never be the best, you'll only build a successful company, not a great one. If you become the best at something, you'll never remain on top if you don't have intrinsic passion for what you are doing. Finally, you can be passionate all you want, but if you can't be the best at it or it doesn't make economic sense, then you might have fun, but you won't produce great results." [20]

SOAR makes *Good to Great* operational. It provides a step-by-step approach to involve those who have a stake in the success of turning a company from good to great by having conversations and input around critical questions that move an organization to greatness. **When participants finish a SOAR process, they can summarize for anyone what the organization does and why, what the future direction is, how they will get there, what needs to be done, and what their particular contribution means to the overall success.**

In the next chapter, we'll explore how to SOAR using the 5-I approach of Initiate, Inquire, Imagine, Innovate, and Inspire to Implement.

Key Points of this Chapter

- Provided examples of strategic questions that can be used in either a "quick SOAR" or more rigorous strategic planning process.
- Provided an illustration of a quick SOAR.

Strategic Thoughts

- Think about a project or opportunity you have; how might you start using SOAR with a quick SOAR application?
- What are key SOAR questions that you might ask at your next planning meeting to start a conversation that aims for building a strengths-based strategy?

Quick SOAR Sample Agenda

TIME	WHO	TOPIC	COMMENTS/METHODS
30 min	Facilitator & all	Strengths intro & breakout	Introduction (5 min), discussion (25 min)
40 min	Teams	Strengths report outs	5 minutes per team (table). 50 participants @ 7 tables = 35 min
5 min	Facilitator & all	Strengths debrief	What did we learn? What does it mean? What will we do about it?
15 min	Sr. Leader	Opportunity knowledge leveling	Sr. leader provides insight into trends, issues, and forces. Presentation & discussion
30 min	Teams	Team opportunity breakout	Team discusses opportunities and adds insights. Reframes challenges
40 min	Teams & facilitator	Report out & opportunity mapping	5 minutes per team (table). 50 participants @ 7 tables = 35 min
5 min	Teams	Opportunity debrief	What does it mean? What will we do about it?
30 min	Facilitator & all	Aspirations intro & breakout	Introduce aspirations. Breakout 5 min, small group discussion 25 min
45 min	LUNCH	LUNCH	LUNCH
40 min	Teams	Aspirations report outs	5 minutes per team (table). 50 participants @ 7 tables = 35 min
40 min	Facilitator & all	Aspirations debrief	What did we learn? What does it mean? What will we do about it?
30 min	Facilitator & all	Results introduction and breakout	Introduce results breakout (5 min), small group discussion (25 min)
40 min	Teams	Results report outs	5 minutes per team (table). 50 participants @ 7 tables = 35 min
40 min	Facilitator & all	Results debrief	What did we learn? What does it mean? What will we do about it?

Chapter 4

How to SOAR using the 5-I's

We will either find a way,

or make one.

— Hannibal

Through our practice with SOAR, we have found a 5-I approach to be useful especially when the goal is to deliver a formal strategic plan. The acronym SOAR describes "what" we are looking for to create the results that are envisioned when we continuously work at what we do best. This chapter is "how to do" SOAR through the 5-I approach. The 5-I stands for Initiate, Inquire, Imagine, Innovate, and Inspire to Implement. We want to stress that there is no one right way to SOAR. It is scalable and flexible. We have found that using the 5-I approach helps make the process flow well whatever the number of participants and time allotted.

On the following pages are descriptions of the five phases.

1. Initiate

2. Inquire

3. Imagine

4. Innovate

5. Inspire to Implement

1. Initiate: *Choosing to SOAR*

During the first phase, the organization's leadership decides whether or not to use the SOAR framework. If they decide to go forward they typically follow these next steps:

- Identify the representatives for the strategic planning team who begin to make the planning decisions. This is sometimes referred to as the core team.
- Identify the number of stakeholders needed to gain a whole system perspective.
- Plan how you will gather the information for the strategic plan. Will it be a two to three-day strategic planning summit? Will it be a one-day strategic planning session? How will you bring the stakeholders into the process? If some cannot attend the scheduled session, who can bring their perspective into the plan?
- What choices and constraints need to be defined and communicated?
- Identity the questions to ask the participants.

An organization's global Human Resource (HR) function considered using SOAR for a unit level strategic plan. An outside facilitator guided a discussion with the following questions:

- How have prior strategic plans been created and executed? Is there a need for greater innovation and alignment?
- What should we keep, extend, and/or stop doing within the HR function?
- Who are the stakeholders that should be directly involved in the strategy process? If not personally participating, how do we make sure all stakeholders are represented in the strategic conversation? How do we communicate their involvement?
- What are the core team's strengths and experience in strategic planning?
- What do we hope to gain from using the SOAR framework?
- When and where do we conduct the strategic conversations?
- What data needs to be readily available for the session?

The questions may vary but the intent of the Initiate phase is to have leadership understand and commit to the SOAR approach to strategic planning and begin to plan the logistics of how information will be gathered for the strategic plan and who will be included.

2. Inquire: *Asking the SOAR questions*

In this phase, participants engage in conversations in small groups or one-to-one interviews using questions created by the core team and/or the executive team. These questions may be similar to the samples listed on pages 16 to 17 or reflect topics identified in the Initiate phase. These conversations and report-outs to the larger group inform the collective group about shared values, aspirations, organizational strengths, opportunities for growth, and definitions of success. This common frame of reference provides grounding for the entire group and establishes the foundation to launch the next phase, Imagine.

In the global HR organization's planning process, strategic questions (listed on pages 16 to 17 in Chapter 3) were asked of approximately forty employees in a two-day session. The questions and conversations were designed to achieve a shared understanding without creating "groupthink."[21] To begin the Opportunity inquiry, HR Leadership provided their insights with an overall view of external trends, corporate response, and how it might affect HR's goals. The observations from the conversations were made visual on mind maps and flip charts and then posted so that shared understanding could be built upon in the next phase, Imagine.

The size of the group and the questions asked will vary, but the intent of the Inquire phase is to create a common understanding of the group's strengths, opportunities, aspirations, and possible results. This common understanding lets the group use their imagination to consider what "might be" in the Imagine phase.

3. Imagine: *Creating a shared vision*

In this phase, small groups meet to engage in "possibility thinking." The goal is to imagine what might happen if they apply the information from the Inquire phase to envision a desired future. Participants imagine the possible future of the organization as it considers the union of strengths, opportunities, and aspirations. Participants are encouraged to be as creative and innovative as possible to visualize a future of actions that reflect high potential opportunities, and the values and aspirations of the community.

The small group to large group conversation flow used in the Inquire phase is again employed. This phase can be accomplished in a short amount of time (one to two hours), since this should be intuitive, top of mind, and encourage breakthrough thinking. A facilitator records and collects the ideas and themes from the reports. A consolidated report is then made available to the whole group. These tangible images and supporting dialogue create the inspiration and excitement to translate strategic vision into coordinated plans and action in the next phase, Innovate.

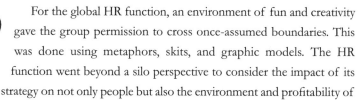

For the global HR function, an environment of fun and creativity gave the group permission to cross once-assumed boundaries. This was done using metaphors, skits, and graphic models. The HR function went beyond a silo perspective to consider the impact of its strategy on not only people but also the environment and profitability of the organization. The group found that the Imagine phase was the one that most engaged the heart and spirit of the participants and produced the energy for the next phases.

In the Imagine phase, the facilitator continually reminds the group of the organizational strengths, opportunities, aspirations, and results so they can refer to them and use them as the foundation for the next phase, Innovate, which will establish strategic initiatives.

4. Innovate: *Designing the strategic initiatives*

This phase transforms creative ideas into action items. The participants work to capture the possibilities identified by the Imagine phase and transform them into strategic initiatives and action items. Because every organization has limited resources, choices must be made. Therefore, prioritization and design of the best possibilities take place. The leadership team might need to clarify or remind the group of the organization's priorities and available resources. Then the group can work within those guidelines to create their recommendations. These recommendations are then forwarded to the leadership team, who will make the final decisions.

The core planning team arranges the initiatives into projects that often require changes to existing processes, systems, structures, and culture. These changes are carefully designed to take advantage of the identified strengths, opportunities, and aspirations in order to get results.

This phase was referred to as "Get Creative, then Get Real" at the global HR function. The openness of the Imagine phase was used to identify all possibilities. The Innovate phase prioritized those possibilities into the vital few initiatives and projects that would have the most impact. For each of the initiatives, the participants considered what changes to processes, structures, systems, and culture would be needed to ensure action and results.

The Innovate phase takes the dream or vision from Imagine and creates a path to realize the vision. This is done through conversations that look at what processes, structures, systems, or culture need to be created or changed. We refer to this as *walking the diamond*, which is shown on the next page. The Innovate phase creates the blueprint or plans that are prioritized for the Inspire to Implement phase.

Walking the Diamond

5. Inspire to Implement: *Going from possibilities to inspired action*

Ultimately, plans require action to lead to success and this phase focuses on action. The energy and commitment from prior phases create the momentum to inspire the completion of the actions to achieve results. Meaningful and measurable goals are defined and the results are then used as feedback measures for any needed course corrections as the plan moves forward. Implementation involves many stakeholders with different skills working on linked projects.

For the global HR unit, the projects were further clarified using "charters." The charters were then translated to performance management objectives for individuals and teams. Scoreboards were created to visibly track the results of the project work and provide feedback, recognition, and celebration. They called this "Sustainability through Visibility." The SOAR approach went beyond producing great ideas to actually create results because time and attention were taken to incorporate the change into the HR business plan and into each employee's Individual Development Plan.

What gives the 5-I process so much impact is the original power and inspiration generated by the Inquire conversations. Those conversations thread through all the phases connecting everyone to the why and how; therefore, they are motivated, indeed inspired, to act. The rewards are many: financial returns, an engaged and productive workforce, and new thinking that leads to new products and market differentiators that define the uniqueness of the organization.

We want to emphasize that SOAR goes beyond just producing great ideas. **SOAR transforms the way people in organizations think and work.** Once organizations open themselves to an inclusive way of working, they are capitalizing on the strengths everyone brings. An upward spiral of positive momentum is created which is self perpetuating over time. In the next chapter, we will illustrate the SOAR framework and the 5-I approach with an in-depth case study.

Inspire to Implement (R)
To achieve Results

Innovate (A)
To reach Aspirations

Imagine (O)
The Opportunities

Inquire (S)
Into Strengths

Initiate
The choice to use

Key Point of this Chapter

- Provided insight and examples of the 5-I approach using SOAR as a strategic planning and implementation approach.

Strategic Thoughts

- How might you introduce SOAR framework and the 5-I approach to create a strategic plan?
- What will people want and need to know before getting started?
- What is the best way to build buy-in and momentum?

Chapter 5

Putting it All Together

A Case Study of SOAR – Haverwood Healthcare

A leader is best when people barely know he exists. When his work is done, they will say: we did it ourselves.

— Lao Tzu

Haverwood Healthcare[22] is a mid-sized regional provider of post-acute services, including nursing homes, assisted living, and rehabilitation services. Each year the company's senior management team sequestered themselves in a hotel to develop the strategic plan for the coming year. They had been using a SWOT-based approach to strategic planning. During a typical strategic planning session, top management reviewed their prior year's goals, objectives, strategies, plans, and policies. From that they would develop new goals and objectives for the coming year. Heavy emphasis was placed on the areas where the company missed their budget and financial projections and discussions about "what went wrong." This annual ritual centered on a SWOT analysis and setting goals and a budget to support it.

Review the Mission

The traditional first step in this ritual was to review the current strategic position of the organization. It began with a broad overview of the company's financial statements and discussion of the existing mission statement. The mission statement provided a purpose or function for the organization — the reason for which the organization exists. Haverwood Healthcare's mission is to *be a quality provider of diversified healthcare services by:*

- *Emphasizing high standards of performance and integrity that will enhance the quality of life of our residents.*
- *Providing our employees opportunities for growth through participation, achievement, recognition, and reward.*
- *Maintaining a strong economic base through sound practices in support of these goals.*

The *mission statement* answers the questions: "Who are we and what business are we in?" A mission statement, which emphasizes the present state of the business, is most effective when developed with a *guiding vision statement,* which answers the question, "Where do we want to be in the future?" The senior management team had created the following vision statement before using SOAR: *To be the long-term healthcare provider of choice in our market areas.*

Review the goals

The next step in Haverwood Healthcare's strategic planning process was to review existing goals. *Goals* refine open-ended statements about such wishes as "being profitable" or "achieving growth in the long-term care market" by defining specific measures. In strategic planning language, goals with measures are often called *objectives*. For example, Haverwood Healthcare's objective was to improve bottom line profitability by 20% in five years. This is a quantifiable statement about a desired strategic goal. Next, Haverwood Healthcare senior management team evaluated the effectiveness of strategies. A *strategy* is simply the "how to" means to achieve the objectives. Strategies are often defined by level. For example:

- *Corporate: Should we grow, maintain status quo, or exit?*
- *Unit: How do we uniquely contribute? What is our competitive advantage? How do we sustain ourselves in the marketplace?*
- *Functional: What should each functional area do to align with the unit and corporate level strategies?*

Haverwood Healthcare operated from the traditional SWOT model. Despite top management's annual strategic planning session and their future looking vision statement, goals and objectives, the reality at Haverwood was that the management group rarely thought about the future strategic direction of the company and what it meant to its 2,800 employees, residents (customers), and community stakeholders. The healthcare market is highly dynamic with constantly evolving competitive, environmental, and legislative changes.

Haverwood was proficient at reacting to outside stimuli and was operating on the assumption that if the daily operations were at a break-even point, the future would take care of itself.

1. Initiate: *How shall we work together?*

For years the company had taken a defensive posture in their markets, working hard to maintain a solid footing in the communities in which they operated. Even when a center did not meet the desired vision of being the provider of choice, the company often maintained it for fear that alternative actions like closing the facility might cause more problems. However, during a recent strategic planning session, it became clear that one of the assisted living facilities had been operating at a deficit for three years and did not meet the company's objective for profitability nor was it a center of *choice*. Senior management felt that they had to face the difficult decision of whether to continue investing significant resources in an attempt to turn the center around or sell it.

A review then showed that for the past several years, the center had been steadily losing market share and was currently operating at 75% of bed capacity. This particular assisted living center also had a unionized staff. The staff's attitude towards the center's management team could best be described as tolerant. Investment would mean less money available for some of Haverwood's more profitable centers, while divestiture could mean loss of market share, stirring up regulatory issues, attracting negative press, angering families and residents, and damaging the company's statewide reputation.

To help analyze the difficult decision of potentially closing a center, the company decided to bring in a consulting firm to develop a facility-level strategic plan at this center. Their hope was to facilitate positive change by first bringing the center to a break-even point and then operating it at a profit. After conducting a search, the company's senior management team selected a firm who would use SOAR for the strategic planning process at the center. What they liked about this framework was that it would bring the facility's staff, management, residents, and family members together as a unified team to create a strategy at the facility. They also hoped that the process would help build a positive working culture. Bringing these stakeholders together was important because SOAR would address diverse factors that inhibited the center's growth: management and staff relations, census development (revenue), and resident (customer) satisfaction. In many ways, this was a final attempt to get everyone working together toward improving the center's bottom line and reputation while creating the most preferred future.

The consultants initiated the process by meeting with the center's management team and identifying a core team of people from various stakeholder groups, including management, staff, residents, and family members. Haverwood's vice-president of market development served on the team as the representative of the company's top management. During the six-week process, facilitated by the consultants, this small core team would identify and involve relevant stakeholders to develop an appropriate strategy for the struggling center.

2. Inquire: *What are our strengths and opportunities?*

Once the core planning team was identified, the consultants worked with the team to create the following questions that would become the basis for the Inquire phase:

* Why did you join Haverwood Healthcare? How long have you been with Haverwood Healthcare? What is your role and contribution(s)?
* Describe a rewarding experience or high point during your employment with Haverwood Healthcare. This would be a time when you felt most proud and excited about being part of our organization.
* What is it that you value about yourself, the nature of your work, the people you work with, and the residents?
* When your facility is operating at its best, what are the core *strengths* that give *life* to this center, without which the center would cease to exist?
* What are the *opportunities* for this facility? How can we best serve the residents? What potential do you see?
* What are the *aspirations* of your department? What image do you have for our facility? What would you like our future to look like?
* What are the *results* that we can measure? What results are most meaningful to you? How will we know we have accomplished something?

The core group created a list of the stakeholders and divided them into small groups of three to five people. Then, the above questions were slightly adapted for use with the residents and their family members. Members from the core team met with each small group and used the questions to create the conversation. During this, the Inquire phase, particular attention was paid to ensure that all stakeholder groups were represented, and the team openly discussed the possibility that the facility might be closed or sold.

Because SOAR purposefully asks positive questions, the small group interaction tends to generate a significant amount of energy, discussion, and collaboration. This was true in the Haverwood case. In fact, the center's Executive Director commented that, "I'm amazed at how willing the staff was to participate and was thrilled with how engaged they became in the discussion. We definitely got off on the right foot. As soon as we started asking questions, they became noticeably more relaxed and quickly started sharing wonderful stories about their experiences with the center. There is no question that this energy carried us through the remainder of the strategic planning process."

3. Imagine: *What can we aspire to?*

Next, the consultants shared the findings with the larger group. The larger group used the findings as a basis to have conversations to imagine the future of Haverwood Healthcare five years from now. They identified the following insights:

STRENGTHS: *Exceptional care, long-term resident loyalty, and a culture of daily appreciation for each other including the staff and residents.*

OPPORTUNITIES: *Provide superior flexible dining service and a daily activity program that engages residents, family members, and local community members.*

ASPIRATIONS: *Be the first choice as local provider as a result of the highly qualified, trained and caring staff that creates radiance and energy in the residents' lives.*

RESULTS: *Increase census by 10% within 30 days and train the entire staff on the importance of census development and their role in contributing to this goal.*

The core team also created a tagline that was adopted by the rest of the employees at the facility: *caring people, caring for people.*

4. Innovate: *What can we create to achieve our aspirations?*

This phase included a series of meetings with specific groups having expertise and interest to help identify specific strategic initiatives needed to strengthen and achieve the opportunities and aspirations identified during the Imagine phase. For instance, in an effort to realize the opportunity of "superior flexible dining service" the following activities took place:

- A resident council was created to allow residents direct input into meal selection and dining times.
- Outside vendors were brought in and training programs were conducted to improve meal quality.
- Monthly in-services were instituted for all dietary staff.
- A café service was set up to allow residents access to snacks during off hours.
- Restaurant style meals were incorporated, including a menu ordering process.

Each of these activities requires new processes or project plans and a point of contact so someone would be held accountable. Those decisions were made in the Implement phase.

5. Inspire to Implement: *How do we move forward to achieve our goals?*

Each new initiative created in the Innovate phase was assigned a team, a timeline, and measurable goals in the Implement phase. For example, in order to implement the "superior dining services," the chef took the lead and he included those stakeholders that were part of the dining experiences, from the staff and food suppliers to the residents and their family members. In addition, each team was required to measure success and report back to the overall team. The measures were based upon one or more defined criteria, for example, dining experience, food quality, customer satisfaction or census growth.

This feedback was used to assess whether the progress was sufficient to achieve the initiative or if further steps were needed. The staff recognized that the successful implementation was highly dependent on maintaining the relationship connections made during the Inquire, Imagine, and Innovate phases and building on the energy and participation of all stakeholders. The progress of the strategic initiatives was communicated to all of the interested stakeholders in an effort to keep them informed, inspired, and engaged. Within six weeks there were five significant results.

1. The center experienced an increase in new residents of 12%.

2. Monthly in-service training was reinstated for all staff on all shifts.

3. The assisted living center became a community gathering place where young members from the community interacted with the seniors.

4. Various departments developed a new spirit of cooperation in serving the residents.

5. Ninety days after the intervention the staff voted to remove the union. The administrator of the facility stated, "We have seen a dramatic shift from a defensive posture of fear from our employees to a new level of excitement about our ability to truly make the facility into what we want it to be while considering each and every stakeholder."

A Positive Divestiture

At this point, one could say that the SOAR intervention was a success. However, the story does not end here. Eighteen months later, the state reduced its reimbursement for this type of healthcare facility, making it no longer viable to operate the center. The company made the decision, for the first time in its history, to take the bold step of closing one of its centers due to this significant uncontrollable change in its external environment.

In its 15-year history, Haverwood Healthcare had never closed a facility. This story is different from many strategic planning stories, because instead of resulting in a happy ending or creating amazing long-term financial returns, it resulted in a positive divestiture. It illustrates that strategic planning does not always end in finding new ways to grow a company. However, as a result of using this approach, Haverwood was more resilient and better able to handle the reality of closing down a center. Closing an assisted living center, which residents consider their home, is not a simple task. Because the staff, residents, families, and management had the opportunity to work together collaboratively to create a strategy and keep the facility open for the previous eighteen months, they took this as an opportunity to plan a strategy and smooth transition to close it down. From the date the closure was announced until the last resident moved out was less than 30 days. Several noteworthy points include the following:

- During the entire transition every staff member showed up for work,
- No one left his or her position prematurely,
- The company worked to find employment opportunities for every employee who desired it, and
- Every resident was placed without incident.

The State Ombudsman who worked with the center during the closure remarked, "The closure was a model of cooperation, participation, and efficiency."

Because of this successful divestiture, Haverwood went on to use the SOAR framework at its regional and corporate level. In the words of Haverwood Healthcare's Vice President of Business Development, "There is no doubt that the divestiture went as well as it did as a direct result of the work we had done previously using SOAR. The SOAR framework created a dialogue among the stakeholders and received positive buy-in from all stakeholders. We weren't just managers and staff doing a job. We were a community of people working collaboratively to do what was best for our residents. What SOAR offers is a strengths-based framework and positive approach to strategy. It provided us an effective and flexible framework that fosters the energy, creativity, and engagement of all our employees and residents."

In the next chapter, we provide additional snapshots of case studies to show the flexibility and scalability of SOAR applications.

Key Point of this Chapter

- This chapter provided a detailed example of a SOAR 5-I approach to create a strategic plan for a healthcare facility.

Strategic Thoughts

- How would you introduce SOAR to your team or organization?
- Who would be part of your core team – the strategic planning team?

Chapter 6 An Invitation to SOAR

All dreams come true if we have the courage to pursue them.

— Walt Disney

SOAR is flexible and scalable; each organization can design its own approach to fit its needs and culture. For example, SOAR was used to coordinate work and ideas among twenty-five federal agencies that had never worked collaboratively before. The federal information technology (IT) community was being called upon to think differently, to find new IT solutions that further good government and make it more accessible to its citizens.

SOAR was used at a three-day off-site with ninety-seven IT leaders from the federal government agencies. It was the first time the representatives of those agencies were in the same room working across agencies to share information and to discover how to strengthen the government's IT infrastructure. SOAR created a collaborative framework, which resulted in an increased level of participation and a positive shift in energy in the room. Based on this experience, the participants reported that they could now envision working together differently in the future. One person said, "Now when there is a question, we should default to sharing." The meeting led to high-level plans that became business cases that incorporate the best ideas from the employees in these federal agencies. People left with a mission and renewed sense that they can make a contribution. They experienced a path to re-make government from the inside out using the best practices learned from each other.

SOAR Snapshots

We are often asked, who has used SOAR and with what results? The answer is a wide variety of organizations around the world at the corporate, business unit, and operating unit levels. SOAR has also been used to: complete environmental scans of an organization's internal strengths and external opportunities; revisit or create organizational values, vision, and mission; formulate strategy; write actual plans; and bring about transformational change. Examples from for-profit, non-profit, and government sectors have been provided throughout this book. In addition, snapshots of other examples are provided below. Our goal is to give you a sense of the many types of organizations and situations where SOAR has been successful and increase your confidence to try SOAR.

1. *A functional department aligns to a new enterprise strategic direction*

ORGANIZATION	**Functional area of a large global manufacturer**
SITUATION	The functional department needed to respond and align to a major change from a focus on organizational efficiency to growth.
APPROACH	5-I SOAR was used with 20 participants for two days that ultimately engaged 75 employees in nine project teams.
OUTCOME AND LESSONS LEARNED	They identified three aligned initiatives and ten projects that engaged all interested employees on project teams. Employees connected with the enterprise changes and created cross department learning communities.

2. *An organization desired to grow and to become more proactive*

ORGANIZATION	**Mental health clinic**
SITUATION	The clinic needed an innovative strategic plan that was more proactive and compelling than its previous strategic plans. The Mental Health Clinic was losing government funding and the need for mental health services was increasing.
APPROACH	5-I SOAR was used with twenty-five participants.
OUTCOME AND LESSONS LEARNED	Stakeholders, especially board members and front line staff, were engaged in a strategy formulation that aligned with the goals. A stretch goal for a five million dollar campaign was recommended and supported by the board. A new culture of philanthropy is being adopted.

3. *A school community needed to respond to a crisis*

ORGANIZATION	**K-12 school district with multiple school locations**
SITUATION	Several schools had been placed on the No Child Left Behind (NCLB) Watch List. The school district wanted to engage and involve stakeholders from the beginning to speed effective implementation. Ongoing community involvement was also critical. The project teams were aligned to the Baldrige quality schools effort. The structures and systems of the Baldrige approach afforded a perfect match to SOAR's strategic focus and ability to quickly impact a culture for positive change.
APPROACH	Quick SOAR and a strategic planning summit followed. Focus groups and communications were offered in English and Spanish.
OUTCOME AND LESSONS LEARNED	Ten project teams with 300 members worked collaboratively on the goals and created five strategic initiatives to get the school system back on track. The schools came off the Watch List within ten months. There was double-digit improvement in fifteen schools.

4. *A new division needed an aligned strategic plan*

ORGANIZATION	**Automotive supplier technology division**
SITUATION	The division needed to create a sustainable enterprise business model to work with Original Equipment Manufacturers to drive business and provide revenue growth for the corporation. The division was operating in silos with no shared vision or strategy for growth.
APPROACH	5-I SOAR approach guided the strategic planning process.
OUTCOME AND LESSONS LEARNED	The division created a vision and mission and identified strategic initiatives, strategies, and goals that aligned with the corporation. New product, service, and market opportunities were identified based on distinctive capabilities. The approach delivered a strategic plan and removed the silos among the three departments in the division. The session created a profitable and collaborative work environment within the Technology Division and corporate headquarters. SOAR was later introduced at the corporate level.

5. *An organization desired a positive and successful merger*

ORGANIZATION	**A recently merged metropolitan and suburban library system**
SITUATION	The Library System was emerging from a merger that had been challenging. They needed to develop a comprehensive and high engagement strategic plan that would guide the organization and its members for the next three years.
APPROACH	A Quick SOAR was used as input for an Appreciative Inquiry (AI) Summit involving over 100 participants from various libraries.
OUTCOME AND LESSONS LEARNED	Six strategic initiatives and 20 goals were identified for the next three years. The board members and employees became highly engaged in the process. Innovation and healing came from hearing many and diverse stakeholder voices. The effort has been so successful that the Library System is engaging in round two. Members of the Library system are utilizing SOAR for their own strategic planning efforts.

6. *A transitioning governance board wanted to develop into a high performance leadership team*

ORGANIZATION	**A professional association governance board**
SITUATION	A highly functioning leadership team was needed to integrate new and old board members in strategic planning and strengths-based team building.
APPROACH	5-I SOAR with Visual Graphic Recording were used to engage the team in action planning and strategic dialogue. SOAR was used as an iterative process for strategic exploration, visioning, and action planning.
OUTCOME AND LESSONS LEARNED	The board identified eight strategic initiatives and designed two action plans. The combination of SOAR and visual graphics allowed the team to do more in less time. SOAR helped the team engage in a deeper strategic dialogue about possibilities. This created more alternatives and enhanced the strategic planning process. There was an effective integration of the new and old board.

7. *An agency required restructuring and outsourcing*

ORGANIZATION	**Large government agency with 17 departments**
SITUATION	The agency needed to engage all employees to create a strategy to outsource a major service. It also needed to relocate other employees or provide outplacement services. This allowed the restructuring of the existing departments to deliver the mission of the agency.
APPROACH	5-I SOAR followed by several planning sessions.
OUTCOME AND LESSONS LEARNED	There was an increase in government efficiency through outsourcing to private industry. The agency achieved greater clarity of accountability and goals. Leadership emerged at all levels by using SOAR.

8. *An individual needed business and life coaching*

ORGANIZATION	**A growth-oriented internet organization**
SITUATION	An executive needed support in a career decision. The issue was to think through the acceptance or rejection of an opportunity to become the director of the Internet organization.
APPROACH	Quick SOAR as a business and life coaching approach.
OUTCOME AND LESSONS LEARNED	The executive decided to accept the position. Through the SOAR process, she achieved a deeper understanding of the organization's and her potential. As director, she turned the organization in a new direction and has strengthened its international role. SOAR is a powerful approach for individual and organizational planning.

These snapshots demonstrate that SOAR is best used by organizations where strategy is not just an annual review of budgets, goals, and objectives nor is it a quarterly financial ritual. Instead SOAR is a 21st century strategic framework that engages the whole system. It is designed for agility and responsiveness. SOAR should be thought of as a process that provides a working framework allowing stakeholders to connect, reconnect, and adjust to real time feedback. It is a way for thinking and learning to be incorporated at every level of an organization.

By using SOAR's strengths-based whole system approach to strategic planning, we have personally been privileged to experience many and varied organizations rekindling their positive core and re-energizing their stakeholders. **SOAR sustains the values of an organization while honoring the knowledge, capabilities, and spirit of its members. Being part of bringing organizational members' spirit back to their work is an unquantifiable personal benefit.**

Every time we have guided an organization or coached colleagues through SOAR, we have been guided as well. The SOAR framework has become part of our DNA. It is hard to imagine any future action or plan without considering where it is strong, what the opportunities are, what we really want to happen, and what would indicate progress and success. As problems and challenges are presented, reframing the problem and looking for the opportunity has become automatic. Implementing SOAR should be tailored to the specific situation and culture. **In sum, SOAR is flexible in its application so that anyone can make strategy part of his or her job.**

We hope you have also been inspired and that you accept the invitation to SOAR!

[1] In his video, *Celebrate What's Right with the World*, Dewitt Jones advocates using a positive mindset to deal with change. He also says "connect with a vision that opens us to possibilities and gives us the courage to soar." For more information visit http://www.dewittjones.com or http://www.starthrower.com/dewitt_jones.htm.

[2] For more information on Appreciative Inquiry (AI), please visit the AI Commons at http://appreciativeinquiry.case.edu/. The AI Commons offers resources and practical tools on AI and the rapidly growing discipline of strengths-based positive change.

[3] To read more on how to transform your organization differently than routine change programs refer to Isern, J. & Pung, C. (2007). Driving Radical Change. *The McKinsey Quarterly*, #4, pp. 1-12.

[4] *Merriam-Webster's Collegiate Dictionary* (10th ed.).(1993). Springfield, MA: Merriam-Webster.

[5] Ibid.

[6] Stavros, J. & Sprangel, J. (2009). Chapter 2: SOAR from Mediocrity of Status Quo to the Heights of Global Sustainability. In C. Wankel & J. Stoner (Eds.), *Innovative Approaches to Global Sustainability*. New York: Palgrave Macmillan Publishers.

[7] Laszlo, C. (2008). *Sustainable Value: How the World's Leading Companies are Doing Well by Doing Good*. Stanford, CA: Stanford Business Books.

[8] Buckingham, M. & Clifton, D. (2001). *Now, Discover Your Strengths*. New York: Free Press and Rath, T. & Conchie, B. (2009). *Strengths-Based Leadership*. New York: Gallup Press.

[9] Clifton, D. & Harter, J. (2003). Investing in Strengths. In K. Cameron, J. Dutton & R. Quinn (Eds.), *Positive Organizational Scholarship* (pp. 111-121). San Francisco, CA: Berrett-Koehler Publishers.

[10] Daly, A., Millhollen, B., and DiGuilio, L., (2007). SOARing Toward Excellence in an Age of Accountability: The Case of the Esperanza School District. *AI Practitioner*. www.aipractitioner.com

[11] Fredrickson, B. (2009). *Positivity: Groundbreaking Research Reveals How to Embrace the Hidden Strength of Positive Emotions, Overcome Negativity, and Thrive*. New York: Crown Publishers.

[12] Dutton J. & Ragins B.R. (2006). *Exploring Positive Relationships at Work,* (p. 5). New Jersey: Erlbaum Publishers.

[13] The search for *positive meaning* has been proposed as a universal human need in the works of Baumesiter & Vohs (2002), Frankl (1959), and Grant (2007) as cited in K. Cameron (2008). *Positive Leadership: Strategies for Extraordinary Performance*, (pp.67-68). San Francisco, CA: Berrett-Koehler Publishers.

[14] Cameron, K. (2008). *Positive Leadership: Strategies for Extraordinary Performance*, (p. 70). San Francisco, CA: Berrett-Koehler Publishers.

[15] Cameron, K. & Lavine, M. (2006). *Making the Impossible Possible: Leading Extraordinary Performance: The Rocky Flats Story*. San Francisco, CA: Berrett-Koehler Publishers.

[16] Isern, J. & Pung, C. (2007). Driving Radical Change. *The McKinsey Quarterly*, #4, p. 3.

[17] This question is from *Good to Great*. Collins, J. (2001). *Good to Great: Why Some Companies Make the Leap ... and Others Don't*. New York: HarperCollins Publishers Inc.

[18] Ibid.

[19] For more information on how to engage large systems see Holman, P., Devane, T. & Cady, S. (2007). *The Change Handbook*. San Francisco, CA: Berrett-Koehler Publishers.

[20] Collins, J. (2001). *Good to Great: Why Some Companies Make the Leap ... and Others Don't*, (p. 97). New York: HarperCollins Publishers Inc.

[21] Groupthink is a term that Irving Janis coined. It means that a group has begun to think alike in order to avoid conflict. Irving Janis (1972, 1982), *Groupthink: Psychological studies of policy decisions and fiascoes*. Boston: Houghton Mifflin.

[22] Haverwood Healthcare is not the real name of this company.

RECOMMENDED BOOKS ON STRATEGY

Bryson, J. (2004). *Strategic Planning for Public and Nonprofit Organizations: A Guide to Strengthening and Sustaining Organizational Achievement, Third Edition*. San Francisco: Jossey-Bass.

Buckingham, M. (2005). *The One Thing You Need to Know about Great Managing, Great Leading, and Sustained Individual Success*. New York: Free Press.

deKluyver, C. & Pearce, J. (2009). *Strategy a View from the Top*, Third Edition. Upper Saddle River, NJ: Pearson Prentice Hall.

Kaplan, R. & Norton, D. (2001). *The Strategy-Focused Organization*. Boston, MA: Harvard Business School Press.

Kim, C. & Mauborgne, R. (2005). *Blue Ocean Strategy: How to Create Uncontested Market Space and Make Competition Irrelevant*. Boston, MA: Harvard Business School Press.

McKinsey Quarterly & The McKinsey Review at www.mckinsey.com.

Mintzberg, H., Lampel, J. & Ahlstrand, B. (2005). *Strategy Safari: A Guided Tour through the Wilds of Strategic Management*. New York, NY: The Free Press.

Mintzberg, H. (1994). *The Rise and Fall of Strategic Planning*. New York, NY: The Free Press.

Porter, M. (1980). *Competitive Strategy: Techniques for Analyzing Industries and Competitors*. New York, NY: The Free Press.

Thompson, A., Strickland, A. & Gample, J. (2008). *Crafting and Executing Strategy,* Sixteenth Edition. New York: McGraw-Hill Irwin.

Sun Tzu (1971). *The Art of War*. Oxford University Press.

A vision is set by a core set of values.
A mission is defined by a vision.
Goals and objectives are defined by a mission.
Strategies are set based on the goals and enabling objectives.
A plan requires a strategy.
Actions move forward from a plan.
Change requires action!

— *Jacqueline M. Stavros*

About the Authors

Jacqueline Stavros, DM has 20 years experience in strategic planning, marketing, international, and organization development and change. Jackie is an Associate Professor for the College of Management, Lawrence Technological University, where she teaches and integrates strengths-based practices like SOAR, Appreciative Inquiry, and sustainable development concepts in her courses: Leading Organizational Change, Strategic Management, and Organization Development.

She has worked and traveled to over a dozen countries in Asia, Europe, and North America. Clients have included: ACCI Business System, BAE Systems, Fasteners, Inc., General Motors of Mexico, Jefferson Wells, NASA, Girl Scouts USA, gedas International, Orbseal Technologies, Tendercare, United Way, as well as many automotive suppliers, nonprofit organizations, and higher education institutions.

She has co-authored and edited many books, book chapters and articles including: *Dynamic Relationships: Unleashing the Power of Appreciative Inquiry in Daily Living* (with Cheri Torres) and *The First Appreciative Inquiry Handbook: for Leaders of Change* (with David Cooperrider and Diana Whitney), and the third edition of *Practicing Organization Development: A Guide for Leading Change.*

She earned a Doctorate in Management at Case Western Reserve University, an MBA from Michigan State University, and a BA from Wayne State University. Jackie is an associate for the Taos Institute. She is a board member of the Positive Change Core, a virtual global organization that focuses on strengths-based approaches to learning in primary education (Pk-12th grade). She is a member of the Academy of Management, Organization Development Network, and the Organization Development Institute. Contact her at jstavros@comcast.net

Gina Hinrichs, Ph.D. is founder and president of Hinrichs Consulting, L.L.C., which provides business management consulting for continuous and sustainable improvement. During the last 25 years, Gina has worked in engineering, operations, marketing, and project management. She has led many workshops and projects to achieve shifts in performance and process improvement. Gina consults with a range of organizations from education and social profit organizations to companies with $20 billion in sales. She works with

Acknowledgments

IBM, John Deere, Schneider National, ProHealth Care, Quad City Bank & Trust, U.S. Cellular, Library Systems, Community Action organizations, and multiple schools systems. Her career and client experience combine to provide a rich understanding of organizations and processes to facilitate change.

She has co-authored and edited several book chapters and articles including: *The Fieldbook for Collaborative Work Systems* and *The Handbook of High-Performance Virtual Teams*. She is working on a new book called, *It takes a Community: Strength-focused Transformation for Schools*.

Gina has earned a Ph.D. in Organization Development, an MBA from Northwestern University, Master's in Organizational Behavior, a BA in History, and a BS in Engineering. Gina is an adjunct professor of management for Capella University, Lawrence Technological University, and Benedictine University and is a past editor of OD Journal. She teaches management courses combining strategy and organization development theory, critical thinking, and practical experience to prepare emerging business leaders.
Contact her at ghinrichs517@gmail.com

No book is the product of its authors alone. This book is no different. Creating such a thin book takes a great deal of time, effort, and depth of conversations with many people.

We are tremendously grateful and want to thank the early thinkers and readers who have helped to shape SOAR: Major Loyd Beal III, Kim Cameron, Daniel Christopher, David Cooperrider, Frank A. Cusmano, Tom Griffin, Tom Heinrichs, Lisa Herrig, Barb Hyder, Jim Jenkins, Jackie June, Lynn Kelley, Ed Kimball, Paul Larson, Bob Lees, Leslie Light, Deborah Maher, Patricia Malone, Roberta Peirick, Pat Pinkston, Cheryl Richardson, Clarence Rivette, Dan Saint, Jane Seiling, Tony Silbert, Joe Sprangel, Marge Schiller, Cheri Torres, Jane Watkins, Susan Wood, and Teresa Woodworth. Thank you to the anonymous reviewers whose ideas and editorial advice strengthen this book.

We acknowledge the helpful insights and feedback from the students at Lawrence Technological University's College of Management who provided thoughtful critiques and suggested applications of SOAR.

We would especially like to thank our editor Sue Hammond who read out loud to us every sentence in this book until we got it right! Thank you for your direction, commitment, patience, and support.

Specials thanks to our husbands, Paul Stavros and John Hinrichs, who both provided critical reviews. And we thank our families and friends for their support and patience during the long writing and editing hours.

We are grateful to all of you!

I love the stories in this book and wished that I had a book like this to order for all my employees. SOAR offers a way of being in a relationship to the organization. An organization lives in the mind of employees and the results come from an employee's way of thinking, planning, and acting. SOAR is a thought starter to think positive about strategy and new program potentials to inspired action.

Tom Heinrichs, Retired Manager of Training and Development,
Healthcare Services Organization,
Grosse Pointe, Michigan

Without engaging the hearts and aspirations of your teams and employees, your business cannot achieve its real potential. The future of your business depends on every employee – at every level – giving all that they have and doing all that they can. SOAR provides a means to invite everyone into the success of the business and ensures the alignment required to compete in a global market.

James R. Jenkins

In a few short pages, Jackie Stavros and Gina Hinrichs, both pioneers in the use of an Appreciative Inquiry approach to organization change, manage to shift the reader's perspective from seeing organization change in parts to an understanding of organization change grounded in wholistic thinking – the organization as a living and constantly shifting entity totally connected in ways that require an image of organizations as healthy human systems. Beginning with the well-respected "parts" model for organization change called SWOT (strengths, weaknesses, opportunities and threats) these two exceptionally innovative and creative women, grounded in a more wholistic view of human systems, have managed to take a very useful and often successful SWOT process and shift the focus from dichotomy to wholeness. The process so articulately and powerfully described in this valuable *Thin Book* is called SOAR (strengths, opportunities, aspirations and results). This shift not only results in useful plans and processes, it also leads to energy and excitement within the system and commitment to creating an organization capable of continuous and generative change in response to today's climate that will tolerate nothing less.

This *Thin Book*, like so many others in this series, is a MUST READ!

Jane Magruder Watkins & Ralph Kelly, Appreciative Inquiry Unlimited
Williamsburg, Virginia

It's amazing the power that can be derived from focusing on the strengths of ourselves and our people. It's also amazing that it surprises us. What could be more natural and more powerful!

Michael A. Rinkus, Senior Vice President, National Group Manager
International Trade Services, Comerica Bank

This book is a must read for everyone engaged in organizational change. The SOAR Framework is brilliant! It simultaneously addresses business management solutions while encouraging collaboration among all stakeholders. I experienced exceptional results after applying SOAR principles in my organization. SOAR is easy to use and offers the holistic, strengths-based, approach to decision making necessary for transformation. Large and complex organizations such as the U.S. Department of Defense will benefit when SOAR is used to affect enterprise transformation.

Major Loyd Beal III, Acquisition Officer, U.S. Army,
Warren, Michigan

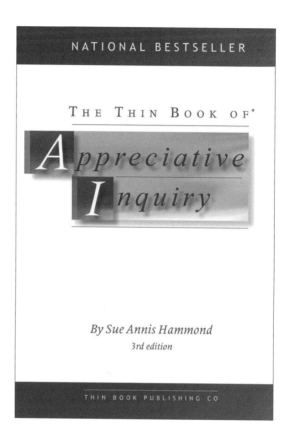

NATIONAL BESTSELLER

THE THIN BOOK OF®

Appreciative Inquiry

By Sue Annis Hammond
3rd edition

THIN BOOK PUBLISHING CO

The Thin Book of ® Appreciative Inquiry is the introduction to
the exciting organizational change philosophy called Appreciative
Inquiry. Appreciative Inquiry is a way of thinking, seeing and acting
for powerful, purposeful change in organizations. The 3rd edition
which has more how-to s and updated research is now available.

Price: $7.95
Paperback: 56 pages
ISBN 978-0-9889538-0-2

THE THIN BOOK OF

Trust

AN ESSENTIAL PRIMER FOR
**BUILDING TRUST
AT WORK**

BY CHARLES FELTMAN

Having the trust of those you work with is too important not to be intentional about building and maintaining it. With this book, you will learn how to build and maintain strong trusting relationships with others, and repair trust when it is broken, by being intentional and consistent in your language and actions. Understanding and consistently demonstrating trustworthy language and behavior will help you earn and keep the trust of the people you work with.

Price: $9.95
Paperback: 68 pages
ISBN: 978-0-9665373-9-0

Thin Book Publishing

Visit **thinbook.com** for product and
ordering information

Contact Thin Book Publishing Co
Email info@thinbook.com
Phone 541.382.7579
Fax 541.317.8606
Address 70 SW Century Dr.
Suite 100-446
Bend, OR 97702

"THE SINGLE MOST UNTAPPED COMPETITIVE ADVANTAGE IS TEAMWORK"

RESULTS

ACCOUNTABILITY

COMMITMENT

CONFLICT

TRUST

Finally a Team Profile that gives your team data to focus their efforts!

CONTACT ME TO PURCHASE THE PROFILE AND RECEIVE EXPERT COACHING ON HOW TO USE IT

SUE ANNIS HAMMOND
THIN BOOK PUBLISHING CO
888.316.9544   sue@thinbook.com

AUTHORIZED PARTNER • ACCREDITED FACILITATOR

THE FIVE BEHAVIORS
OF A COHESIVE TEAM™